A MĀORI PHRASE A DAY

365 PHRASES TO KICKSTART YOUR REO

HĒMI KELLY

RAUPŌ

Hēmi Kelly is of Ngāti Maniapoto and Ngāti Tahu–Ngāti Whāoa descent. He started learning te reo Māori as a young teenager and naturally progressed into teaching roles after study. Hēmi is a full-time lecturer in te reo Māori at the Auckland University of Technology. His academic research and writing focus largely on the revitalisation of the Māori language and translation studies.

Hēmi is a licensed translator and graduate of Te Panekiretanga o Te Reo (The Institute of Excellence in the Māori Language). In 2017, Hēmi translated Witi Ihimaera's novella *Sleeps Standing*, and he published his first book *A Māori Word a Day* in 2018. In 2019, Hēmi published his first creative writing piece in English in *Pūrākau*, a collection of Māori myths retold by Māori writers.

Ngā Wāhanga / Chapters

Kupu whakataki

Introduction

Kia ora!

Welcome to *A Māori Phrase a Day*. This book is a follow-up to *A Māori Word a Day*. Instead of a word a day, it gives you a whole phrase for every day of the year to help extend your knowledge of the Māori language in a range of contexts and situations.

I've divided 365 phrases into 28 common categories that include the different settings and activities we may find ourselves in or doing, day in, day out. Each phrase has the English translation and notes offering alternative words you can use, different ways to answer a question, information about the etymology of a word, or elements of the Māori culture.

I want to acknowledge you for picking up this book and committing to learn te reo Māori. This book is designed to aid you in your learning regardless of whether you're at the beginning stages of your journey or already on the road to fluency. As you continue learning, your confidence in te reo Māori and your overall understanding of the language will grow. I hope you find the phrases relevant and useful and that they extend your ability to express yourself in te reo Māori in a variety of everyday situations.

In order for te reo Māori to live and grow it needs to be spoken everywhere. That's achievable if we start with *A Māori Phrase a Day.*

Kia kaha te ako, kia kaha te kōrero.

Hēmi Kelly

Whakahua

Pronunciation

The Māori alphabet contains five vowels, eight consonants and two digraphs:

a e i o u   h k m n p r t w   ng wh

Each vowel sound is either short or long. Short vowels are written normally (as above), while long vowels are written with a macron to indicate the elongated sound:

ā ē ī ō ū

The difference between the short and long vowels can alter the meaning of the word; e.g. kaka (clothing), kākā (native parrot), or kakā (spicy). Vowels in Māori are pronounced in the same way as the highlighted vowel or letter combination in the following English words:

a	**a**men
e	**e**mpty
i	**e**vening
o	**o**rphan
u	tr**ue**

Consonants are pronounced the same as in English, except for 't' and 'r'. The 'r' is rolled gently, and there are two 't' sounds depending on the vowel that follows – **ti** and **tu** are pronounced with a slight sibilant sound, while **ta**, **te** and **to** are pronounced with a dull sound similar to a 'd'. The 'ng' digraph is pronounced as it sounds in the English word 'winger' and the 'wh' is pronounced like the English 'f' sound.

Ngā tau, ngā rā me te wā

Numbers, dates and the time

Throughout the phrases you'll see the opportunity to talk about time, dates and money. When you learn the phrase, you can refer back to this section to customise your own phrases.

Ngā tau / Numbers

tahi	1	tekau mā tahi	11
rua	2	tekau mā rua	12
toru	3	toru tekau	30
whā	4	whā tekau	40
rima	5	rima tekau mā rima	55
ono	6	ono tekau mā whitu	67
whitu	7	kotahi rau	100
waru	8	waru rau mā tahi	801
iwa	9	iwa rau tekau mā ono	916
tekau	10	kotahi mano	1000

Ngā rā o te wiki / The days of the week

Rāhina	Monday
Rātū	Tuesday
Rāapa	Wednesday
Rāpare	Thursday
Rāmere	Friday
Rāhoroi	Saturday
Rātapu	Sunday

Ngā marama o te tau / The months of the year

Kohitātea	January
Huitanguru	February
Poutūterangi	March
Paengawhāwhā	April
Haratua	May
Pipiri	June
Hōngongoi	July
Hereturikōkā	August
Mahuru	September
Whiringa-ā-nuku	October
Whiringa-ā-rangi	November
Hakihea	December

Ngā wāhanga o te tau / The seasons of the year

Raumati	Summer
Ngahuru	Autumn
Hōtoke	Winter
Kōanga	Spring

Te wā / The time

Kotahi karaka	One o'clock
Rima karaka	Five o'clock
Rima meneti i te rima karaka	Five minutes past five
Tekau meneti i te rima karaka	Ten minutes past five
Hauwhā i te rima karaka	Quarter past five
Haurua i te rima karaka	Half past five
Rua tekau meneti ki te ono karaka	Twenty minutes to six
Hauwhā ki te ono karaka	Quarter to six
Tekau meneti ki te ono karaka	Ten minutes to six

Use *i* for past the hour and *ki* for to the hour

1.

I TE ATA

In the morning

Maranga mai!

Get up! / Rise and shine!

•

Mai following a verb indicates direction towards the speaker, the person or thing central to the utterance. *Maranga mai* usually follows the command *E oho!* (Wake up!).

He rā hou tēnei.

Today's a new day.

●

rā – day

Swap *hou* (new) for other words like *pai* (good), *wera* (hot), or *makariri* (cold).

Kāti te moeroa!

No sleeping in!

●

Kāti means to cease or stop what you're doing.
Change *moeroa* (sleep in) with other verbs like
whakaroaroa (dawdle) or *amuamu* (moan).

I au te moe?

Did you sleep well?

●

moe – sleep

Au is a stative here. It means to be sound (of sleep).

Huakina ngā ārai.

Open the curtains.

●

ārai – curtains

Replace *huakina* with *katia* and you'll have 'close the curtains'!

Kia tere kei tōmuri koe!

Quickly or else you'll be late!

●

Kia kakama and *kia horo* are other ways to tell someone to hurry up.

He aha hei parakuihi māu?

What would you like for breakfast?

•

parakuihi – breakfast

Here are a few options:

He tōhi – Toast
He pata kai – Cereal
He hēki – Eggs
He witipiki – Weetbix
He kore noa iho – Nothing

He kawhe māku.

I'll have a coffee.

●

kawhe – coffee

If you're feeling like something else to drink you
might use one of the following:

tī – tea
tiakarete wera – hot chocolate
wai ārani – orange juice
miraka – milk
ranu pūmua – protein shake

Kua pōkai koe i tō pēke?

Have you packed your bag?

●

pēke – bag

You might respond with:

Āe – Yes
Kāore anō – Not yet
Taihoa – Just a minute

Āwhea koe hoki mai ai ki te kāinga?

When will you come home?

●

āwhea – when (future time)
kāinga – home

Learn the times on page 12 and customise your answer. Add *pea* (maybe, possibly, thereabouts) when you're not certain.

Ā te rima karaka pea – Around 5 o'clock

Kia pai te rā!

Have a good day!

●

You could use another adjective instead of *pai* (good), like *rawe* (amazing) or *haumaru* (safe).

Kia ora – Thanks

2.

I TE RŪMA MOE

In the bedroom

E hoki ki tō rūma!

Go back to your room!

●

rūma – room

E before a verb consisting of one or two syllables
turns the verb into a command; e.g. *E tū* (stand up),
e noho (sit down) or *e hoki* (go back).

Kei te tīwekaweka tēnei rūma.

This room is a mess.

●

You might replace *tīwekaweka* (messy) with other adjectives:

riko – filthy
mā – clean
nahanaha – tidy

Kei te haunga a roto nei.

It's smelly in here.

●

haunga – smelly

Here are other adjectives you could use:

ātaahua – beautiful
mahana – warm
makariri – cold

Huakina te matapihi.

Open the window.

●

te matapihi – the window

Here are some other options:

te kūaha – the door
te whata kākahu – the wardrobe
ngā ārai – the curtains

Kaua e waiho ō taonga i te papa.

Don't leave your things on the floor.

●

papa – floor
taonga – treasure, property, goods

Other options:

pukapuka – books
hū – shoes
kākahu – clothes

Whakahokia ērā ki te wāhi tika.

Put those back where they belong.

●

You might use *ērā* – those (away from the speaker and listener) or *ēnā* – those (near the listener).

Nā wai ēnei?

Who do these belong to?

●

If you're talking about clothing, jewellery or shoes you say 'Nō wai ēnei!' Depending on the subject of the sentence and its association to the owner, use either *a* or *o*.

He aha tēnei?

What's this?

●

Tēnei is the singular of *ēnei*. *Tēnā* refers to something near the listener, and *tērā* is something away from both the speaker and listener.

He pene tēnā – That (near you) is a pen
He kurī tērā – That (over there) is a dog

Hoatu ngā pukapuka ki te paenga.

Put the books on the shelf.

●

paenga = shelf

If there is only one *pukapuka* (book), use *te* ('the' – singular) instead of *ngā* ('the' – plural).

Whakatikahia te moenga.

Make your bed.

●

The suffix -*nga* turns the verb *moe* (sleep) into a noun; *moenga* (bed). *Whakatika* means make it right or straight.

He paraikete anō mōu?

Do you want another blanket?

●

paraikete – blanket

You might respond:

Āe, tēnā koa – Yes, please
E pai ana – It's okay
Ka nui tēnei – This will do

Kaua e noho i te urunga.

Don't sit on the pillow.

●

urunga – pillow

It's frowned on to sit on the pillow since it's where the head rests. The head is the most *tapu* (sacred) part of the body.

Pera is another word commonly used for pillow.

Koia kei a koe mō te whakapaipai.

You're the best when it comes to cleaning up.

●

Use the beginning of this phrase in any context where you're giving praise:

Koia kei a koe! – You're the best!

3.

I TE RŪMA HOROI

In the bathroom

Kei whea te wharepaku?

Where's the bathroom?

●

It's more common to hear *whareiti* among the Tainui iwi. *Paku* and *iti* both mean small, so *wharepaku* translates to the 'small house'!

Kei te haere au ki te wharepaku.

I'm going to the bathroom.

●

wharepaku – toilet, bathroom

There are three singular pronouns – *au* (I/me), *koe* (you) and *ia* (he/she).

Kei te hia mimi ahau.

I need to pee.

●

It's not unusual to explicitly say exactly what you
need to do, especially when dealing with kids. There
are only two options: *mimi* ('pee' or as they say,
'number one') or *tiko* ('number two').

Rakaina te kūaha.

Lock the door.

●

rakaina – to lock

Other options:

huakina – open
katia – shut

Taihoa, kāore e roa.

Hang on, I won't be long.

●

This is a handy phrase to know in case someone is knocking on the *kūaha*.

Kua pau te pepa whēru.

The toilet paper has run out.

●

Swap *pepa whēru* (toilet paper) for other items like *pēniho* (toothpaste), *hopi* (soap) or *hopi makawe* (shampoo).

Tukua te wai.

Flush the toilet.

●

wai – water

This literally means 'release the water' – you get it, given the context, *nē*?

Horoia ō ringaringa.

Wash your hands.

●

Swap *ringaringa* (hands) for other parts of the body, like *makawe* (hair), *taringa* (ears) or *karu* (eyes).

Kei te uwhiuwhi ahau.

I'm having a shower.

●

If you want to talk in the third person, use *a* before the name, e.g. *Kei te uwhiuwhi a Jamie* (Jamie is having a shower).

Kaua e roa rawa.

Don't be too long.

●

The use of *rawa* (too, overly, unduly) after the adjective indicates an unsatisfactory degree of a quality or attribute.

Kei a koe tētahi tāora?

Do you have a towel?

●

tāora – towel

Other options:

paranene – flannel
taitai niho – toothbrush
hopi – soap

Taitaihia ō niho.

Brush your teeth.

●

niho – teeth
taitai niho – toothbrush
pēniho – toothpaste

Whakairihia te whāriki kaukau.

Hang the bathmat up.

●

The *whāriki kaukau* (bathmat) won't become *maroke* (dry) by staying *mākū* (wet) on the floor. You'll also want to hang up your *tāora* (towel).

4.

NGĀ KĀKAHU

Clothing

Nō wai tēnei?

Who does this belong to?

●

Nōku – It's mine
Nōna – It's his/hers
Nōu – It's yours
Nō Tui – It's Tui's

Kei te mā, kei te riko rānei ēnei?

Are these clean or dirty?

●

Kei te mā – They're clean

Kei te riko – They're dirty

Aua – I don't know

Me horoi tēnei hāte.

This shirt needs a wash.

●

hāte – shirt

Me (must, had better, should) is used before verbs to form a command. Remember, you can change *tēnei* (this) to *ēnei* (these) if there is more than one item.

Hoatu ki te mīhini horoi kaka.

Put it in the washing machine.

●

mīhini horoi kaka – washing machine

Kaka is short for *kākahu* (clothes). Some iwi use other words for clothing. In Tainui you hear *pakikau*, in Taranaki you might hear *maemae* and Ngāi Tahu use *weruweru*.

Whakairihia ngā kākahu ki waho.

Hang the clothes out.

•

kākahu – clothes

When the clothes are dry you might ask someone to *tīkina ngā kākahu* (fetch the clothes).

Pōkaingia ngā kākahu.

Fold the clothes.

●

tarau – pants
tīhāte – T-shirt
poraka – jersey
tōkena – socks
tarau kōpū – underwear

Whakahokia ngā kākahu ki ngā hautō.

Put the clothes away in the drawers.

●

hauto – drawers
whata kākahu – wardrobe
paenga – shelf

Whakamātauhia ēnei hū.

Try these shoes.

●

hū – shoes, footwear

You could also say, *kuhuna ēnei* (put these on).

Kei te awhe te panekoti i a koe?

Does the skirt fit you?

●

panekoti – dress, skirt

Respond with:

Āe, kei te awhe – Yep, it fits
Kāo, kāore i te awhe – No, it doesn't fit
Ka aroha – What a pity

He pēwhea ki ō whakaaro?

What do you think?

●

whakaaro – to think (verb); idea, thought, opinion (noun)

Respond with:

Heoi anō – So-so
He pai – It's good
He rawe – It's excellent

Tōrire ana koe!

Looking smart!

●

You could replace *tōrire* (smart) with other words
like *taiea* (classy), *tuu* (elegant) or *huatau* (beautiful).

Me pēwhea ngā kākahu ā te pō nei?

What's the dress code tonight?

●

Me ōkawa – It's formal

Me ōpaki – It's informal

Me tangatanga – It's casual

Kuhuna ngā kākahu tangatanga.

Put on your comfy clothes.

●

You could replace *tangatanga* (loose, comfortable) with *matatengi* (warm, thick) or *karukaru* (old clothes), or try out some of the other words you've already learnt.

5.

I TE KĪHINI

In the kitchen

Kei te hiakai koe?

Are you hungry?

●

Thirsty? Then just replace *hiakai* (hungry) with *hiainu* (thirsty).

He aha tō tino kai?

What's your favourite food?

●

kai – eat (verb); food (noun)

Respond with:

He mīti – Meat
He korare – Greens
He huamata – Salad
He parāoa parehe – Pizza

Māku e tunu.

I'll cook.

●

Here are some options if someone else is going to do the cooking.

Māna – He/she will
Māu – You will
Mā Māmā – Mum will

Māu ahau e āwhina.

You can give me a hand.

●

āwhina – to assist, help

Māku koe e āwhina – I can give you a hand

Tīkina tētahi kōhua.

Grab a pot.

●

kōhua – pot

Or grab a:

pereti – plate
oko – bowl
kapu – cup
koko nui – large spoon
māripi – sharp knife

Waruwaruhia ngā rīwai.

Peel the potatoes.

●

rīwai – potato

Other vegetables include:

kūmara – sweet potato
paukena – pumpkin
kāroti – carrot

Kei whea te pīhore?

Where's the peeler?

●

pīhore – peeler

Other utensils include:

māripi – sharp knife
papa kotikoti – chopping board
tīwara – can-opener
tātari – sieve
muku – dishcloth

Kua pau te hinu.

The oil's all gone.

●

hinu – oil

Other kai include:

pata – butter
puehu parāoa – flour
huka – sugar
pata kai – cereal
miraka – milk

Ka waiho tēnei ki whea?

Where should I put this?

●

You might respond with:

Ki te kāpata – In the cupboard
Ki te hautō – In the drawer
Ki te paenga – On the shelf
Ki te umu – In the oven
Ki te pouaka makariri – In the fridge

Māku e whakamātau.

Let me try (taste) it.

●

whakamātau – to try, to attempt

Kia iti noa – Just a little bit
Kia iti iho – Less than that
Kia nui ake – A bit more

He reka te kai?

Is the food good?

●

reka – tasty

Respond with:

He pai – It's good
He namunamuā – It's delicious
He kawa – It's yuck

Kia nui ake te tote.

It needs more salt.

●

tote – salt

Other condiments include:

pepa – pepper
raukikini – spices
puehu hirikakā – chilli powder

Kua tata rite te kai.

The food is just about ready.

●

rite – to be ready

When *tata* is placed before a verb or stative, it indicates something is very close to reaching a particular state.

6.

I TE TĒPU

At the table

Whakaritea te tēpu.

Set the table.

●

tēpu – table

This would include laying out the *naihi* (knives),
pune (spoons) and *paoka* (forks).

Hoatu ngā kīnaki ki te tēpu.

Put the sauces on the table.

●

kīnaki – sauce, relish

Other condiments include:

kīnaki tōmato – tomato sauce
wairanu huamata – mayonnaise
wairanu – gravy

Kua hora te kai!

Food's up!

●

hora – to be spread out

This is a very common phrase. You might also hear *kai* being used in the plural – *ngā kai.*

Haere mai ki te kai!

Come and eat!

●

Haere mai – Come here! Welcome!

There's a saying for when people dawdle: '*Kotahi te karanga ki te tangata, e rua ki te kurī*' (people are only called once, dogs are called twice). In other words, don't ignore the call to eat!

Whakapaingia te kai.

Bless the food.

●

Here is a small *karakia* (blessing) you could use:

Nau mai e ngā hua
O te wao, o te ngakinga
O te wai tai, o te wai māori
Ko Rangi e tū nei
Ko Papa e takoto nei
Tūturu whakamaua kia tīna
Hui e, tāiki e

E mua kaikai, e muri kai hūare.

First in, first served.

●

This is an old whakataukī (proverb) that literally means 'early arrivals have the pick, but latecomers may only get spittle'.

Kaua e kaihoro, he nui te kai.

Don't rush, there's plenty of food.

•

kaihoro = to eat greedily

Kai (food) is an important part of being hospitable and it's always better to have plenty than not enough.

Kia tika te noho.

Sit properly.

●

Kia is used here to give commands involving adjectives like *tika* (correct, proper). The most commonly known command of this nature would be *kia ora* (be well).

Te reka hoki!

How delicious!

●

Replace *reka* (tasty) with another adjective to say something different: *āwenewene* (sweet), *māhihakiha* (bland) or *totetote* (salty).

Homai te tote me te pepa.

Pass the salt and pepper.

●

Swap out *tote* (salt) and *pepa* (pepper) with any of the below:

pereti – plate
kapu – cup
parehūhare – serviette

Māku e horoi ngā rīhi.

I'll do the dishes.

●

rīhi – dishes

Māna – He/she will
Māu – You will
Mā Hera – Hera will

Mukua te tēpu.

Wipe the table.

●

tēpu – table

The word *ūkui* or *ūkuia* also means 'wipe', but for some tribes you'd only use it for a particular part of the body you'd hope no one would be attending to in the dining room!

Tēnā koe i ō manaakitanga.

Thank you for your hospitality.

●

Manaakitanga is the process of showing respect, generosity and care for others, and as you can imagine, *kai* is a big part of this process.

7.

TE HĀEREERE

Commuting

Mā hea koe haere ai ki te mahi?

How do you get to work?

●

mahi – to work (verb); work (noun)

Respond with:

Mā runga pahi – By bus
Mā runga waka – By car
Mā raro – By foot

Me haere tahi tāua.

We should travel together.

●

haere – to go, travel

kōrua – you two
koutou – you lot
tātou – all of us

Kia tere, kei mahue koe i te pahi!

Quick, you'll miss the bus!

●

mahue = be left behind

Other modes of transport you could miss if you don't hurry up are *waka tere* (ferry), *tereina* (train) and *waka rererangi* (airplane).

Kua kī te waka.

The vehicle is full.

●

It's important to note that in modern Māori *waka* is commonly used for any kind of vehicle.

Kei te wātea tēnei tūru?

Is this seat free?

●

tūru – chair

Respond with:

Āe, kei te wātea – Yes, it's free
Kāo, kāore i te wātea – No, it's not free

Kua tae mai te tereina.

The train is here.

●

tereina – train

Other modes of transport include:

pahi – bus
waka rererangi – airplane
tekehī – taxi

Kei a koe tō tīkiti?

Do you have your ticket?

●

tīkiti – ticket

Respond with:

Āe, kei ahau – Yes, I have it
Aī, kei whea rā? – Darn, where is it?
Kei a koe? – Do you have it?

Koinei taku tūnga.

This is my stop.

●

tūnga – stop, standing place, position

Ka piki au i konei – I get on here
Ka heke au i konei – I get off here

Ringaringatia te pahi.

Wave the bus down.

●

Ringaringa, the word for hand or arm, is also the verb for 'wave'. Adding the suffix *tia* makes it a command.

Kua tono ahau i tētahi waka.

I've ordered a vehicle.

●

tono – to order, request

Replace *waka* with one of the following:

tekehī – taxi
Ūpa – Uber

Kei waho te waka.

The vehicle is outside.

●

waho – outside

Respond with:

Kei te haere atu – I'm going
Kāore e roa – Won't be long
Taihoa – Hang on

Kei te haere ahau ki te taunga waka rererangi.

I'm heading to the airport.

•

Taunga (landing place) and *waka rererangi* (airplane) makes *taunga waka rererangi*. It's long but it makes perfect sense.

Āhea tō rerenga?

When's your flight?

●

Sometimes *rerenga* is shortened to *rere* in this context. Check the times on page 12 to customise your answer. If it's at 3 o'clock, you'd say, *ā te toru karaka*.

8.

I RUNGA
I TE WAKA

In the car

Mā wai e taraiwa?

Who's going to drive?

●

taraiwa – to drive

Māku – I will
Māna – He/she will
Māu – You will
Mā Tadgh – Tadgh will

Kei whea ngā kī?

Where are the keys?

●

kī – key

Respond with:

Kei konei – Here
Kei kō – Over there
Aua – I don't know

Piki mai, e hoa.

Jump in, mate.

●

hoa – friend, mate

You're literally saying 'jump on the vehicle'. *Piki* means 'to climb' or to get on or in.

Ko au ki mua.

I'm in the front.

•

mua – in front

If someone is in the back, you would say, *ko koe ki muri.*

Kua tata pau te penehīni.

We're just about out of gas.

●

Penehīni is a transliteration of the word 'benzine', which is an old word for petrol.

Me whakakī te waka.

I need to fill up.

●

Waka is used to refer to any vehicle. If you want to be specific, here are a few types of waka:

pahi – bus
wakaroa – van
kutarere – scooter
taraka – truck
motopaika – motorbike

Hoatu ngā pēke ki muri.

Put the bags in the back.

●

pēke – bag

Replace *ki muri* with:

ki mua – in the front
ki te papa – on the floor
ki te tūru – on the chair (but not if it's kai!)

Haere tōtika.

Carry on (go straight).

●

Huri whakatemauī – Turn left
Huri whakatematau – Turn right
E tū! – Stop!

Whāia te ara poka.

Take the shortcut.

●

ara – way, path, route

ara roa – long route
ara tōtika – direct route

Whakamahia te mahere i tō waea.

Use the map on your phone.

●

mahere – map, GPS

If you want to say 'use your phone', just say, 'whakamahia tō waea'.

He waewae taumaha tōu.

You've got a heavy foot (You're speeding).

●

waowao   foot, leg

If someone is going too slow replace *waewae taumaha* with *waewae māmā* (light foot).

Kia āta haere.

Go slow.

●

Āta before a verb indicates that the action should be carried out with care.

Arā tētahi tūnga waka.

There's a park.

●

arā – there, over there, there it is, there they are

Change the subject of the sentence by replacing
tūnga waka (park) with one of the following:

toa – shop
hokomaha – supermarket
whare penehīni – petrol station

9.

TE TŪTAKITAKI

Meeting and greeting

Tēnā koe, e hoa.

Hi, mate.

●

Tēnā koe – Hello (to one)
Tēnā kōrua – Hello (to two)
Tēnā koutou – Hello (to three or more)

Kia ora, kei te pēhea koe?

Hi, how are you?

●

Respond with:

Kei te pai ahau – I'm good
Kei te ora ahau – I'm well
Kei te hiakai ahau – I'm hungry
Kei te hōhā ahau – I'm annoyed

Nō hea koe?

Where are you from?

●

You can either answer this question by referencing the place you come from or the tribe you belong to.

Nō Taupō ahau – I'm from Taupō
Nō Ngāti Tūwharetoa ahau – I'm from
  Ngāti Tūwharetoa

Ko wai tō ingoa?

What's your name?

●

ingoa – name

Here's an example response:

Ko Hēmi tōku ingoa – My name is Hēmi

Kua roa te wā!

It's been a long time!

●

wā – time

Kua aua atu te wā! – I don't know how long it's been!

Kei te pai tō āhua.

You're looking good.

●

āhua – appearance

Replace *pai* with:

kino – bad
rawe – excellent
ora – well

Kei te aha koe ināianei?

What are you doing now?

●

ināianei – now

Kei te ako – Studying
Kei te mahi – Working
Kei te whakatā – Taking a break

Kei whea koe e mahi ana?

Where are you working?

●

Use *kei* before the name of the place to say 'at', 'on' or 'in' at the present time.

Kei te whare wānanga – At the university

Me hui anō tāua ākuanei.

Let's meet again soon.

●

ākuanei – soon

Replace *ākuanei* with:

āpōpō – tomorrow
ā tērā wiki – next week
ā tēra marama – next month

Kei te aha koe ā te mutunga wiki?

What are you doing on the weekend?

●

mutunga wiki – weekend

Respond with:

Kei te kore noa iho – Nothing
Kei te mahi – Working
Kei te whakatā – Resting

He aha tō tau waea?

What's your cellphone number?

•

You might hear *tau waea* or *nama waea* being used for phone number.

Māku koe e pātuhi.

I'll text you.

●

pātuhi – text

Replace *pātuhi* with:

waea – call
whakapā – contact
īmēra – email

Hei konā!

See you then!

●

Other common farewells include *ka kite anō* (see you again) and *mā te wā* (see you in time).

If someone is leaving and you are staying you can say *Haere rā* and they might respond by saying *E noho rā*.

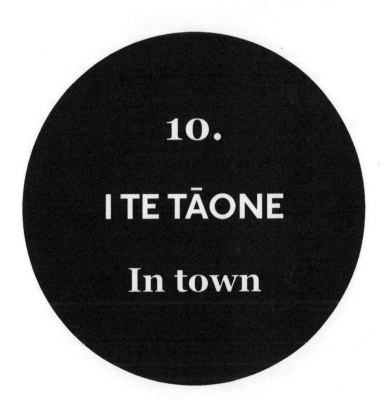

10.

I TE TĀONE

In town

He tokomaha ngā tāngata i te tāone.

There are lots of people in town.

●

tokomaha – a lot of people

Replace *tokomaha* with:

tokoiti – a small number of people

Kua pokea te rori.

The road is busy.

●

Rori is the transliteration of road; more traditional words are *ara* or *huarahi*.

E tū.

Stop.

•

You might know *e tū* to mean 'stand up'. It's also the command to tell someone to come to a standstill when moving.

Me whakawhiti tāua i te rori.

Let's cross the road.

●

whakawhiti – to cross over

Tirohia ngā taha e rua – Look both ways

Kaua e oma – Don't run

Kia āta haere – Go carefully

Taihoa, kia kā te rama kākāriki.

Wait until the light is green.

●

rama   light

Kei te whero tonu te rama – The light's still red

Titiro ki ngā taha e rua, ka whakawhiti ai.

Look both ways and then cross.

●

taha – side, way

te taha matau – the right side
te taha mauī – the left side

Puritia taku ringa.

Hold my hand.

●

ringa – hand

Replace *ringa* with:

pēke – bag
koti – coat
tokotoko – walking stick

Kei te haere au ki te whare pukapuka.

I'm going to the library.

●

whare pukapuka – library

Replace *whare pukapuka* with:

poutāpeta – post shop
whare taonga – museum
pēke – bank
toa – store
kēmihi – chemist

Ka whakahoki au i ēnei pukapuka.

I will return these books.

•

pukapuka – book

Ka is the tense used before verbs when the action is in the future.

Me kimi au i tētahi kēmihi.

I need to find a chemist.

●

kēmihi – chemist

Replace *kēmihi* with:

pēke – bank
mīhini tango moni – ATM machine
whare kawhe – café
wharekai – restaurant
toa hoko hū – shoe shop

E hia te roa i konei ki te pēke tino tata?

How far is it to the nearest bank?

●

konei – here

Respond with:

E rua meneti pea? – Maybe two minutes?
E rima meneti – Five minutes.
Kāore e roa – Not long.

He rawe tēnei toa.

I love this store.

●

toa – shop, store

He pai ki a au – I like it
He iti te utu – It's cheap
He nui te utu – It's expensive

He aha te whāwhai?

What's the rush?

●

Change *whāwhai* (to be in a hurry) to another verb like *whakaroroa* (to delay) or *tatari* (to wait).

11.

I TE AKOMANGA

In the
classroom

He karaehe tāku.

I have a class.

●

karaehe – class

You might add on to the end *ināianei* (now), *ākuanei* (soon) or *ā te pō nei* (tonight).

Tokohia ngā tāngata i tō karaehe?

How many people are in your class?

-

tangata – person
tāngata – people

Respond with:

Tokoiti – Not many
Tokomaha – A lot
Tekau mā ono – Sixteen

Kia kaha te ako.

Go hard learning.

●

ako – to learn or teach

Kia kaha (be strong, get stuck in, keep going) is
very common now. Include the activity by using *te*
followed by the action, *Kia kaha te kōrero*.

Titiro mai, whakarongo mai.

Look and listen up.

●

This old-time favourite can be used in all contexts. It's also part of the *whakataukī* used to encourage learners of te reo Māori: '*Titiro mai, whakarongo mai, kōrero mai*' (look, listen and speak).

Kei a koe tētahi pene?

Do you have a pen?

●

pene – pen

Tētahi (one, a, an) is the singular of *ētahi* and is often followed by a noun but can stand without one.

Kei a au tētahi – I have one

He aha tō tino kaupapa?

What's your favourite subject?

●

kaupapa – subject

Pāngarau – Maths
Pūtaiao – Science
Tōrangapū – Politics
Te reo Pāniora – Spanish

Ko wai tō kaiako?

Who's your teacher?

●

kaiako – teacher

The Māori versions of 'Ms' and 'Mr' are *Whaea* and *Matua*, which mean 'Aunty' and 'Uncle'.

He aha te rā tuku i te aromatawai?

What's the due date for the assessment?

•

aromatawai – assessment

Replace *aromatawai* with:

tuhingaroa – essay
whakamātautau – exam

Kāore anō kia oti i ahau aku mahi kāinga.

I haven't finished my homework.

●

mahi kāinga – homework

Kua oti aku mahi kāinga – I've finished my
   homework.
Kua tata oti aku mahi kāinga – I've nearly finished
   my homework.

He pātai tāku.

I have a question.

●

pātai – to ask (verb); question (noun)

Change *tāku* to *āku* if you have more than one question.

He tika ō whakaaro.

Your ideas are correct.

•

You might change *tika* (correct) to one of the following:

pai – good
rorirori – crazy
hāngai – relevant

Kei te pīrangi āwhina koe?

Do you need help?

●

pīrangi – to need, want

Respond with:

Āe, āwhina mai! – Yes, help me!
Māku koe e āwhina – I'll help you
Ngā mihi – Thank you

Kaua e mate wheke.

Don't give up.

●

These words of encouragement come from a well known proverb that says, 'Kaua e mate wheke, me mate ururoa', which literally means, 'Don't die like an octopus, die like a white shark!'

12.

I TE TARI

In the office

He aha tō īmēra?

What's your email?

●

īmēra – email

Replace *īmēra* with:

tau waea – phone number
Pukamata – Facebook
Paeāhua – Instagram

Māku koe e īmēra.

I'll email you.

●

Or vice versa:

Māu ahau e īmēra – You email me.

Whakautua te waea.

Answer the phone.

●

whakautu – to answer, respond

Ko wai? – Who is it?
Kei konā a Jonathan? – Is Jonathan there?

He hui tāku ināianei.

I have a meeting now.

●

hui – to meet (verb); meeting (noun)

Learn different dates and times to talk about a *hui* you have in the future.

He hui tāku ā te Rāmere – I have a meeting on
　　Friday.
He hui tāku ā te toru karaka – I have a meeting at
　　three o'clock.

Kei te pokea au e te mahi.

I'm swamped with work.

●

poke – to swamp, overcome, inundate

When the suffix -*a* is added to the verb *poke*, the subject is swamped, overcome or inundated by something.

Kei a wai tētahi tēpara?

Who has a stapler?

●

tēpara – stapler

rākau pūmahara – USB stick
pene – pen
pūhihiko – charger

Ki a au tō kutikuti mō te wā poto?

Can I borrow your scissors for a second?

●

kutikuti = scissors

Ki a au literally means 'to me'. You could say, *ki a au tēnā* (pass me that thing near you).

I mau mai koe i ō kai i tēnei rā?

Did you bring lunch today?

●

Kei a au aku kai – Yes, I have my lunch

Me hoko kai ahau – I need to buy lunch

He mahana a roto nei.

It's warm in here.

●

mahana – warm

Replace *mahana* with:

makariri – cold
mātao – freezing

Tēnā koa, tāruatia tēnei.

Photocopy this, please.

●

The word 'please' doesn't exist in Māori as it does in English, but to soften a request just add *tēnā koa* or *tēnā* before it.

Kua pau te pepa i te pūrere tā.

The photocopy machine is out of paper.

●

Your *purere tā* (printer) might also run out of *waituhi* (ink) or *hiko* (power).

Kei te pēhea tō wātea āpōpō?

What's your availability like tomorrow?

•

wātea – to be free, available

Kei te wātea ahau – I'm free
Kāore au e wātea – I won't be free

Māu aku mahi e titiro?

Can you look over my work?

●

Swap *titiro* (to look) with other verbs like *hōmiromiro* (to edit) or *arohaehae* (to analyse).

13.

TE HOKOHOKO

Shopping

Kei te hokomaha ahau.

I'm at the supermarket.

●

hokomaha – supermarket

Replace *hokomaha* with:

toa – shop
tāone – town
tākuta – doctor's
tūranga tereina – train station

He aha tō pīrangi?

What do you want?

●

He tiakarete – A chocolate

He āporo – An apple

He aihikirīmi – An ice cream

He kore noa iho – Nothing

Tīkina tētahi torore.

Grab a trolley.

●

torore – trolley

Replace *torore* with:

rawhi – basket
pēke – bag

I mau mai koe i te rārangi kai?

Did you bring the food list?

●

rārangi kai – food list

Respond with:

Āe, kei ahau – Yep, I have it
Auē, i wareware – Oh no, I forgot it

Torutoru noa iho ngā mea e hiahiatia ana.

We only need a few things.

●

moa   thing

Torutoru (literally, 'two-threes') means a few, while *ruarua* or ('two-twos') means a couple.

Kia hia ngā riki?

How many onions?

●

riki – onion

Respond with:

Kia kotahi – One
Kia rua – Two
Karekau – None

Ka nui tēnā.

That will do.

●

You can also use this idiom to say 'enough is enough'.

E hia te utu o te pata kai?

How much is the cereal?

●

patakai – cereal

Use *e* before numbers *rua* (two) through to *iwa* (nine). As you can see the *e* is omitted before *kotahi* (one) and *tekau* (ten) below.

Kotahi tāra – One dollar
Tekau tāra – Ten dollars
E toru tāra, e rima tekau hēneti – Three dollars and
   fifty cents

He taumaha te utu.

That's expensive.

●

utu – price, cost

He māmā te utu – That's cheap
He pai te utu – That's a good price

Hoatu tēnei ki te pēke.

Put this in the bag.

●

pēke – bag

Replace *pēke* with:

rawhi – basket
torore – trolley

Kaua e wareware te parāoa.

Don't forget the bread.

●

wareware – to forget
parāoa – bread

Or substitute with:

miraka – milk
ngā huawhenua – vegetables
ngā huarākau – fruits

He aha atu anō?

What else?

●

He tīhi – Cheese
He pihikete – Biscuits
He waina – Wine
He pia – Beer
Karekau – Nothing

Māku e utu.

I'll pay.

●

Māna – He/she will
Māu – You will
Mā Ciarán – Ciarán will

14.

I TE WHAREKAI

In the restaurant

Me puta tāua ki te kai.

Let's go out to eat.

●

puta – go out

Respond with:

Kua kai kē ahau – I've already eaten
He whakaaro pai tēnā – That's a good idea
Hoake tāua – Let's go

He rongonui tēnei wharekai.

This restaurant is famous.

●

wharekai – restaurant

Rongo (hear) and *nui* (widespread) equals 'famous', or well known.

Kia tirohia te rārangi kai.

Let's take a look at the menu.

●

rārangi kai – menu

He pai te āhua – Looks good
Kāore e pai – It's not good

He tēpu kei te wātea?

Are there any free tables?

●

tēpu – table

Karekau – Nothing
He nui – Plenty
Whai mai – Follow me

Tokorua māua.

There are two of us.

●

māua – us (me and one other)

Toko- is the prefix used with the numbers two to nine when referring to people.

He aha te tino kai i konei?

What's the most popular dish here?

●

He karikari – A curry
He parāoa parehe – A pizza
He parāoa rimurapa – A pasta
He pākī – Burgers

Māku tēnā.

I'll grab that.

●

He aha māu? – What will you have?
He pai te āhua   Looks good.

He aha tāu i tono ai?

What did you order?

●

tono – to order, request

I tono ahau i te parāoa rimurapa – I ordered the
  pasta

He nui te homai.

What a generous serving.

●

You can put *āhua* or *tino* before an adjective to alter the meaning, like so.

āhua nui – somewhat big
tino nui – very big

Kātahi te kai reka ko tēnei!

This food is absolutely delicious!

●

Swap out *reka* with *mākihakiha* to say it's 'absolutely flavourless!'

He pūrini māu?

Pudding?

●

pūrini – dessert, pudding

Respond with:

Ehara! – Of course!
Tēnā pātai hoki! – What a silly question!
Kāo, kua kī ahau! – No, I'm full!

Kua puta a pito.

I'm as full as a bull.

●

This idiom means that the *pito* (bellybutton) has literally popped out, so you can imagine just how full you've become!

Tukua aku mihi ki te ringawera.

Give my compliments to the chef.

●

ringawera = the cook or kitchen workers

The word literally means 'hot hands'. Some iwi use the term *kanohi wera* or 'hot face'.

15.

I TE PĀPARAKĀUTA

At the bar

Kei te maroke te korokoro.

I'm feeling thirsty.

●

korokoro – throat

Literally, 'my throat is dry'.

He aha hei inu māu?

What do you want to drink?

●

inu – drink

He pia – A beer
He waina – A wine
He wihikē – A whisky
He wai – Water

Māku te haute.

My shout.

●

haute – to treat someone, shout (drinks, etc.)

Māku a tua atu – I've got the next one

Kei a au ētahi pūtea.

I have some cash.

●

pūtea – money

Replace *pūtea* with:

moni – money
ukauka – coins
rau – notes

Kimihia tētahi wāhi.

Find a spot.

●

wāhi – place, spot, location

Kei te wātea a konei? – Is here free?
Kei te wātea tēnei tēpu? – Is this table free?
Kei te wātea ēnei tūru? – Are these chairs free?

Mauri ora!

Cheers!

●

In modern times, the term *mauri ora* (life essence) is often used as the Māori equivalent of 'bon appétit' before eating and 'cheers' before drinking.

He kaha te whana i tēnei.

This has a strong kick.

●

whana – kick

This idiom is used when referring to a strong drink like a long black coffee or a shot of whisky.

He nanakia te pēne.

The band isn't bad.

●

pēne – musical band

Nanakia means to be better than expected, not too
bad, pretty good.

Kua pau taku waina.

My wine is finished.

●

waina – wine

Pau means 'to be consumed, exhausted, used up, finished, spent, depleted'.

Kua āhua haurangi ahau.

I'm a little bit tipsy.

●

haurangi – to be drunk

Waiho ō hoa i te kāinga – Leave your friends at
  home.
Karangahia he tekehī – Call a taxi.

Kia kotahi anō.

One more.

●

anō – again, more

Ka nui tērā – That's enough
Kia kotahi anake – Only one

Kātahi anō ka tō te rā!

It's still early!

●

tō – to set (of the sun)

You might hear this when someone is trying to convince someone to stay later; it means 'the sun has only just set'.

Tonoa he kai timotimo.

Order a snack.

●

Kai (food) and *timotimo* (to nibble) make *kai timotimo* (snack).

16.

I TE RŪMA NOHO

In the lounge

Whakakāngia te pouaka whakaata.

Turn on the TV.

●

pouaka whakaata – TV

Here are some other options:

pūmahana – heater
pūrerehau – aircon
rama – light

Tēnā, homai te roumamao.

Pass the remote, please.

●

roumamao – remote

Homai – Give me
Hoatu – Give away
Hoatu te roumamao ki a Pāpā – Give the remote to
  Dad

He aha tēnei hōtaka?

What's this programme?

●

hōtaka – programme

Replace *hōtaka* with:

kiriata – film
pakiwaituhi – cartoon
pakipūmeka – documentary

Me mātaki tāua i te aha?

What should we watch?

●

tāua – me and you

If you're in a group of three or more people use *tātou*.

Koinei taku tino kiriata.

This is my favourite film.

●

When *tino* is used before a noun it indicates that that thing is top or unrivalled.

Kāore au e pai ki tēnei kiriata.

I don't like this film.

●

Kāore au e mārama ki tēnei kiriata – I don't
understand this film.

Whakawhitihia te hōngere.

Change the channel.

●

hōngere – channel

Respond with:

He aha ai? – Why?
He hōhā tēnei hōtaka – Because this programme is
 boring

Whakaitihia te reo.

Turn down the volume.

●

reo – voice, volume

Replace *whakaitihia* with:

whakakahangia – turn up
whakangūtia – mute

Katia ngā ārai.

Shut the blinds.

●

ārai – curtain, blind

Huakina ngā arai – Open the blinds

Haere mai ki te noho i te hāneanea.

Come and sit on the couch.

●

Change *te hāneanea* (sofa, couch) to *tōku taha* ('next to me' or literally 'by my side').

Tīkina tētahi paraikete mō tāua.

Grab us a blanket.

●

paraikete – blanket

Change *mō tāua* (for me and you) to *mōku* (for me)
or *mō māua* (for me and my mate).

Kaua e noho noa, he mahi tāu.

Don't laze around, you have work to do.

•

Kāti te noho noa – Stop lazing around

Whakatikahia te rūma noho.

Clean up the lounge.

●

Ruma noho and *nohomanga* both mean lounge or living room

17.

I TE PŌ

At night

E hoki ki te moe.

It's time for bed.

●

moe – to sleep

Literally, 'return to sleep'.

Mihi atu ki te whānau.

Say goodnight to the family.

●

whānau – family

Respond with:

Pō mārie, e te tau – Goodnight, my darling
Hei āpōpō – See you tomorrow
Kihi mai – Give me a kiss

Kuhuna ō kahumoe.

Get into your pyjamas.

●

kahumoe – pyjamas

The word *kuhuna* means 'to get into' or to put on.

Takoto mai.

Lie down.

●

takoto – to lie down

Add *i tōku taha* to say 'next to me'.

Kei te mahana koe?

Are you warm?

●

mahana – warm

Replace *mahana* with:

pai – okay
wera – hot
makariri – cold

Ka oho moata ahau āpōpō.

I have an early start tomorrow.

●

oho – to wake up

Moata is early in the morning. For early to a meeting, use *wawe* instead.

I tae wawe ahau ki te hui – I arrived early for the meeting.

Kua whakaritea te pūoho?

Have you set the alarm?

●

pūoho – alarm

If you want to include the time you could add *mō te ono karaka* (for six o'clock). See page 12 for telling the time.

Whakatata mai.

Come in close.

●

whakatata – go close to

Awhi mai – Hug me
Kihi mai – Kiss me
Piri mai – Keep close

Kia hia ngā pukapuka?

How many books (do you want)?

●

If you want two books, say, *Kia rua ngā pukapuka.*

E moe ō karu.

Close your eyes.

●

Depending on the speaker, you might hear other words for eyes, like *whatu*, *kamo* or *kanohi*.

Whakawetongia te rama.

Lights out.

●

whakawetongia – turn off

Rama and *raiti* are transliterations of the words 'lamp' and 'light'.

Replace *whakawetongia* with:

whakakāngia – turn on

Kia au te moe.

Sleep tight.

●

au – be sound (of sleep)

Replace *au* with:

roa – long
pai – good

Hei te ata.

See you in the morning.

●

ata – morning

Depending on who you're talking to, you could
add on at the end, *e te tau* (my darling), *e hoa* (my
friend), *e taku tama* (my boy), or *e taku kōtiro* (my
girl).

18.

TE HUARERE

The weather

Kei te aha te huarere?

What's the weather doing?

●

huarere – weather

You might also hear, *kei te pēhea te huarere?* (how's the weather?).

Te āhua nei ka paki.

It looks as though it's going to be fine.

●

te āhua nei – it looks as though

Ka paki – It will be fine
Ka ua – It will rain
Ka whiti te rā – The sun will shine

Tōna tikanga ka ua.

It's meant to rain.

●

ua – rain

Replace *ua* (rain) with *paki* (fine), *kāpuapua* (cloudy) or *huka* (snow).

Kei te pupuhi te hau.

It's windy.

•

hau – wind

You could add a word to *hau* (wind) to describe
the type of wind – *hau maiangi* (light wind) or *hau
pūkeri* (strong wind).

He rangi wera tēnei.

It's hot today.

●

rangi – day

Replace *wera* with:

hāuaua – rainy
hauhau – windy
kāpuapua – cloudy

E rua tekau mā whā te paemahana.

It's twenty-four degrees.

●

paemahana – temperature

Check out the numbers on page 10 to customise your phrase.

Pakaru mai ana te ua.

It's raining cats and dogs.

●

Pakaru mai ana implies that something is coming in bucketloads or large quantities. For example, *pakaru mai ana te kata* (laughing like a hyena).

Kuhuna ō kamupūtu.

Put your gumboots on.

●

kamupūtu – gumboots

Or put on your:

koti ua – raincoat
koti matatengi – thick coat
pōtae – hat, beanie

Auē, ka mahue taku hari hamarara!

Oh no, I should've brought an umbrella!

●

hamarara – umbrella
hari – bring, take

Auē is a good one to know. Depending on the
situation and the way it's said, it can mean many
things: 'Heck!' 'Oh dear!' 'Oh no!' 'Shit!' . . . I'll stop
there.

He āwhā kei te haere mai.

There's a storm brewing.

●

Swap *āwhā* (storm) for another word to show what the weather has in store for us, like *rangi paihuarere* (fine day).

Kua mahea te rangi.

The sky has cleared.

●

mahea – clear

Rangi and *rā* are both words for day. *Rangi* is derived from the name Ranginui (Sky Father).

Kua mao te ua – The rain has cleared
Kua pārīrā te hau – The wind has ceased

Kei te mahana haere te huarere.

The weather is getting warmer.

●

When *haere* follows a verb, it indicates gradual change or increase in a state.

Nau mai te raumati!

Bring on summer!

●

nau mai – welcome
raumati – summer

Replace *raumati* with:

ngahuru – autumn
hōtoke – winter
kōanga – spring

19.

I WAHO O TE WHARE

In the backyard

E puta ki waho tākaro ai.

Go outside and play.

●

Replace *tākaro* (play) with another verb like *oma* (run), *umere* (yell) or *pekepeke* (jump).

Kuhuna tō pōtae.

Put your hat on.

●

pōtae – hat

Replace *pōtae* with:

koti – jacket
poraka – jersey
tarau – pants

E piki i te rākau.

Climb the tree.

●

rākau – tree

You might also need, *e heke i te rākau* (get down from the tree).

Kia kaha te pekepeke.

Jump as hard as you can.

●

You can replace *pekepeke* (jump) with other activities like *oma* (run), *whiu* (throw) or *whana* (kick).

Whiua mai te pōro.

Throw me the ball.

●

pōro – ball

Whanaia mai te pōro – Kick the ball to me

Kia tūpato, kei hinga koe.

Be careful, you might fall over.

●

tūpato – careful

Hinga is to fall over from a standing position. If you wanted to say 'fall down' (from a height) use *taka* instead.

Me tohatoha koe i ngā taonga.

You should share your things.

•

tohatoha – to share

taonga – treasures, toys, property

Replace *taonga* with:

taputapu – equipment

takawairore – toys

Me tauomaoma tātou.

Let's have a race.

●

Replace *tauomaoma* (race) with other activities like *tauhunahuna* (hide and seek) or *hanga whare* (build houses).

Ko koe te toa!

You're the winner!

●

toa – winner

You can replace *koe* with another pronoun or the name of whoever won:

au – me/I am
ia – he/she is
Koro – Koro is

Whakahokia ngā taonga katoa.

Return all the toys.

●

katoa – all, every

Me mahi tahi tātou.

Let's all work together.

●

mahi tahi – to work together
tātou – all of us

Replace *tātou* with another pronoun:

kōrua – you two
koutou – all of you
tāua – you and I

Kua pau te hau.

I'm exhausted.

●

hau – wind, breath

This is a good idiom to use when you've run out of energy, or if something no longer works.

Hoki mai ki roto!

Come back inside!

●

Kei te ua – It's raining
Kei te tō te rā – The sun's going down
Kei te makariri haere – It's getting cold

20.

I TE MĀRA

In the garden

Tuatahi ka kauhuri i te oneone.

First we need to turn the soil.

●

oncone – soil

Tua- is a prefix used with numbers one to nine to form ordinals, that is, to indicate a sequence or ranking system, e.g. *tuarua* means 'second'.

Whakatōkia tētahi kākano.

Plant a seed.

●

kākano – seed

Whaka- is prefixed to adjectives, statives and verbs to cause something to happen or to be.

Kei te matewai ngā tupu.

The plants are thirsty.

●

tupu – grow (verb); plant (noun)
matewai   thirsty

You might already know the word *mate* which means 'dead' or 'death'. If *mate* is joined to a noun like *kai* or *wai*, it indicates a desire, need or want for that thing.

matekai – hungry

Riringihia ki te wai.

Sprinkle it with water.

●

riringi – to pour out

Have you noticed that some river names start with *wai*? In these cases, the river's name describes the nature of its water, e.g. Waimakariri (cold water), Waimahana (warm water), Waikato (flowing water).

Hei te toru marama ka hauhake i ngā huawhenua.

We'll harvest the vegetables in three months.

●

hauhake – to harvest
huawhenua – vegetables (fruit of the land)
huarākau – fruit (of the tree)

Kua maoa ngā kōhia.

The passionfruit are ripe.

●

maoa – be ripe
kōhia – passionfruit

Other *huarākau* include:

pītiti – peach
āporo – apple
ārani – orange

Whatiia mai ētahi huarākau.

Pick some fruit.

●

whatī – to pick (fruit)

Adding the suffix *-ia* turns this verb into a command. Replace *huarākau* (fruit) with one of the following:

rōpere – strawberry
purūpere – blueberry
parakipere – blackberry

Raua atu ki te kete.

Put them in the kit.

●

kete – kit

This is another example of a passive command using the suffix -*a* attached to the verb *rau* (to put into).

Ngakia mai ngā tarutaru.

Pull out the weeds.

●

ngaki – to clear (weeds)
ngā tarutaru – the weeds

Whakamahia te koko.

Use the shovel.

●

koko – shovel

Replace *koko* with:

kāheru – spade
purau – rake
pāketu – garden hoe

Me tipi te pātītī.

The lawns need mowing.

●

pātītī – lawn
tipi – cut, mow

Pōtarotaro is 'lawnmower'.

Ka pai ō mahi.

Good work.

●

Take it to another level by saying, *tau kē ō mahi!* (excellent work!)

Katohia mai ētahi putiputi mā Māmā.

Pick some flowers for Mum.

●

putiputi – flower

Check out the waiata *He putiputi koe i katohia* by Apirana Ngata. It likens a loved one to a flower being picked.

21.

I TE TAIAO

In the outdoors

I puni mātou i te ngahere i tērā mutunga wiki.

We went camping in the bush last weekend.

●

puni – to camp
i tērā mutunga wiki – last weekend

Replace *i tērā mutunga wiki* with:

i tērā marama – last month
i tērā tau – last year

Titiro ki tērā manu!

Look at that bird!

●

manu – bird

Replace *manu* with:

rākau – tree
mea – thing
kapua – cloud

Ko whea tērā maunga?

What's the name of that mountain?

●

maunga – mountain

You could replace *maunga* (mountain) with *awa* (river), *roto* (lake), *hiwi* (ridge) or *kāinga* (settlement) to ask the name of a landmark.

Kei te waipuke te awa.

The river is in flood.

●

awa – river

Wai (water) and *puke* (rise up, swell) make *waipuke*
(flood).

He whenua mārakerake tēnei.

This is open country.

●

whenua – land, country
mārakerake – open, clear

Replace *mārakerake* with:

ururua – overgrown
papatahi – flat
pukepuke – hilly

Whakatūria te tēneti.

Put the tent up.

●

tēneti – tent

Add a location – *ki konei* (here), *ki konā* (there, by the listener) or *ki korā* (over there).

Kāore e roa ka tō te rā.

The sun will set soon.

●

kāore e roa – it won't be long, soon

Tahuna te ahi.

Light the fire.

●

ahi – fire

Just make sure you have a *whakaaetanga* (permit) first!

He kaputī mā wai?

Who wants a cup of tea?

●

kaputī – cup of tea

Here are some keywords:

tīraurau – teabag
wai wera – hot water
kapu – cup

I mau mai koe i te matira?

Did you bring the fishing rod?

●

matira – fishing rod

Replace *matira* with:

aho – line
mōunu – bait
matau – hook

Āpōpō ka puta ki te hī ika.

Tomorrow we'll go out fishing.

●

hī ika – to fish with a hook and line

Here are some other future times to replace *āpōpō*:

Ā te Rāhoroi – On Saturday
Ā te mutunga wiki – On the weekend
Ā tērā wiki – Next week

Kua puta mai ngā whetū.

The stars are out.

●

whetū – star

Other heavenly bodies include:

te marama – the moon
ngā aorangi – planets
ngā kāhui whetū – star constellations

Whakarongo ki te ruru e koukou ana.

Listen to the morepork hooting.

●

ruru – owl, morepork

In Māori, there are verbs that represent the cries of individual native birds. This is illustrated in the following whakataukī:

Ka koekoe te tūī, ka ketekete te kākā, ka kūkū te kererū

(The tūī sings, the kākā chatters and the kererū coos)

22.

NGĀ WHANAUNGATANGA

Relationships

Ko wai tō ingoa whānau?

What's your family name?

●

ingoa – name

Ko Emery tōku ingoa whānau – Emery is my family
name

Nō Te Kōpua tōku whānau.

My family is from Te Kōpua.

●

You could use a place name or an iwi name to say where your family come from; e.g. *Nō Ngāti Maniapoto tōku whānau.*

He nui tōku whānau

My family is big.

●

You might replace *nui* (big) with one of the following:

āhua nui – somewhat big
tino nui – very big
iti – small

He rerekē mātou katoa.

We're all different.

●

Rerekē (different) or *ōrite* (similar, alike).

He tuāhine ōu?

Do you have any sisters?

●

There are four different words in Māori we use to
describe our sibling relationships.

tuahine – sister (of a brother)
tungāne – brother (of a sister)
tuakana – older sibling (same gender)
teina – younger sibling (same gender)

Ko au te pōtiki o te whānau.

I'm the youngest in the family.

•

pōtiki, mātāmuri – youngest child

mātāwaenga – middle child

mātāmua – oldest (first) child

He huatahi ahau.

I'm an only child.

●

Hua ('fruit' or 'progeny') and *tahi* (one) make
huatahi.

Kua mārena māua ko taku hoa.

My partner and I are married now.

●

Mārena is the common word for marry or marriage. However, traditionally the word *moe* (to sleep) was used and still is today, e.g. *Kua moe rāua* (They're married).

E hia te roa e piri ana?

How long have you been together?

●

E rua rā – Two days
E rua wiki – Two weeks
E rua tau – Two years

Tokohia ō tamariki?

How many children do you have?

●

tamariki – children

You might respond:

Karekau – None
Kotahi – One
Tokorua – Two

He mōkai āku.

I have pets.

●

mōkai – pet

Some *mōkai* include:

ngeru – cat
kurī – dog
honu – turtle
manu – bird
rāpeti – rabbit

He pai ō hoamahi?

Do you have good workmates?

●

Hoa is the word for 'friend'. This word takes on different meanings depending on the word it precedes.

hoariri – enemy
hoa tāpui – close friend
hoa rangatira – spouse
hoa tākunekune – lover
hoa kaipakihi – business partner

He tangata pai tōku rangatira.

My boss is a good person.

●

The *rangatira* was the high-ranking chief in traditional Māori society. Today many people possess the skills and attributes of a *rangatira*.

23.

TE WHAKARITE HAERENGA

Travel plans

E haere ana koe ki whea?

Where are you going?

●

E haere ana ahau ki te hararei – I'm going on holiday

E haere ana ahau ki Te Whanganui-a-Tara – I'm
going to Wellington

Āwhea koe haere ai?

When do you leave?

●

āwhea – when (of future time)

You might respond:

Ā te pō nei – Tonight
Āpōpō – Tomorrow
Ā te Rāmere – On Friday

Ka taraiwa, ka rere rānei koe?

Are you driving or flying?

●

taraiwa – to drive

Tēnā pātai hoki! – What a silly question!

E hia te roa o tō haerenga?

How long is your trip?

●

haerenga – trip, journey

Adding the suffix -nga to the verb *haere* (go, travel) turns it into the noun *haerenga* (trip, journey).

Me pōkai au i taku tueke.

I need to pack my bag.

●

tueke – luggage, bag, suitcase

Replace *tueke* with:

aku kākahu – my clothes
aku hū – my shoes
aku whakakai – my jewellery

Kei a koe tō pūhihiko?

Do you have your charger?

●

pūhihiko – charger

Repace *pūhihiko* with:

uruwhenua – passport
wāreti – wallet
tīkiti – ticket

Mā hea koe haere ai?

Which way will you go?

●

Mā Taupō – Via Taupō
Mā Ahuriri – Via Napier
Mā Ōtautahi – Via Christchurch

Haere mai i tōku taha.

Come with me.

●

Hoatu koe – You go (without me)
Hoake tāua – Let's go (together)

Whakahokia mai he taonga māku.

Bring me back a present.

●

Tahi rā koe! – You're cheeky all right!
Engari mō tēnā! – Not a chance!

Kia nui ngā whakaahua.

Take heaps of photos.

●

whakaahua – photo

You might upload your *whakaahua* on:

Pukamata – Facebook
Paeāhua – Instagram
Atapaki – Snapchat

Kia pai te haerenga!

Have a good trip!

●

Change *pai* (good) to another adjective like *rawe* (amazing) or *haumaru* (safe).

Ka kite anō i a koe ākuanei.

See you soon.

●

This farewell is usually shortened to *Ka kite*. While grammatically incorrect, it's become a well-known colloquial saying.

Haere rā!

Farewell!

●

You might see this when travelling through towns throughout Aotearoa.

Haere rā – Goodbye (said by the person staying)
E noho rā – Goodbye (said by the person leaving)

24.

TE KAUKAU

Swimming

He rangi pai tēnei mō te kaukau.

It's a good day to go swimming.

●

kaukau – to swim

Change *kaukau* (swim) to another activity depending on the weather:

hīkoi – walk
oma – run
noho i te kāinga – staying indoors

Kuhuna ō kahu kaukau.

Put your togs on.

●

kahu kaukau – togs

Other beach gear includes:

tāora – towel
mōwhiti kaukau – goggles
kārewa – floaty

Kia mau ki te kārewa.

Hold on to the floaty.

●

kārewa – floaty

Kia mau ki a au – Hold on to me
Kia mau ki a Pāpā – Hold on to Dad

Kua pari te tai.

The tide is in.

●

tai – tide

Kua timu te tai – The tide is out

Kia tūpato i te au.

Be careful of the current.

•

au – current (of water)

This can be used at the river or the beach.

Kaua e tawhiti i te tahatika.

Don't go too far from the shore.

●

tawhiti – far away

tahatika – the water's edge (of a river, lake or shore)

Kei te mahana te wai.

The water is warm.

●

wai – water

Replace *mahana* with:

wera – hot
makariri – cold
mātao – freezing

E ruku ki raro i te wai.

Dive under the water.

●

raro – under, below

E ruku! – Dive! But *Kia tūpato!* (Be careful!)

Kaukau mai.

Swim this way.

●

kauhoe tāwhai – freestyle
kau apuru – breaststroke
kau kiore – backstroke

He tohunga koe ki te kaukau.

You're an expert at swimming.

●

tohunga – expert

He autaia koe – You're pretty good
He tino pai koe – You're very good

Haere mai ki te pāinaina.

Come and catch some rays.

●

Pāinaina means to warm yourself by the fire, or to dry off or bask in the sun.

Pania tō mata ki te ārai tīkākā.

Put sunscreen on your face.

●

mata – face

Ārai (block out, prevent) and *tīkākā* (sunburn) make *ārai tīkākā*.

Me hanga whare onepū tāua?

Shall we build a sandcastle?

●

whare onepū – sandcastle

You will need the following:

pākete – bucket
kāheru – spade
koko – shovel

25.

NGĀ HĀKINAKINA

Sports and recreation

Kei te tākaro pā whutupaoro mātou.

We're playing touch rugby.

●

pā whutupaoro – touch rugby

Replace *pā whutupaoro* with:

poitarawhiti – netball
poitūkohu – basketball
poiwhana – soccer
whutupaoro – rugby

He aha te wā o te kēmu?

What time's the game?

●

kēmu – game

Respond with:

Kotahi karaka – One o'clock
Rua karaka – Two o'clock
Kua tīmata kē – It's already started

Ko wai kei te tākaro?

Who's playing?

●

tākaro – to play

Te Kapa Ōpango – The All Blacks
Te Kapa Kaponga – The Silver Ferns
Te Kapa Pango Tāroaroa – The Tall Blacks

Kāore e kore ka toa koutou.

No doubt you will win.

●

kāore e kore – no doubt

Respond with:

Koirā te whāinga – That's the goal
Koirā te tūmanako – That's what we're hoping for
Mā te wā e tohu – Time will tell

Karawhiua mō te hemo tonu atu!

Give it your all!

●

Watching from the sidelines? Get behind your team with words like *rutua* (tackle), *whiua* (pass it), *whanaia* (kick it), *tukua* (let it go)!

Kai a te kurī!

Bugger!

●

And then there's the expletives! *Kai a te kurī* literally means 'food of the dog'. Just remember, it's one thing to swear when the ball is dropped and another to swear at the person who dropped it!

Kia tau te rangimārie.

Keep your cool.

●

rangimārie – peace, peacefulness, harmony

Kia kaha te mahi tahi.

Do your best to work together.

●

mahi tahi – to work together, collaborate

This phrase can also be used in any context where you want to encourage team work.

Ko wai i toa?

Who won?

●

Ko wai atu? – Who do you think?
Ko Te Kapa Ōpango – The All Blacks
I haupārua – It was a draw

E hia te tapeke?

What was the score?

●

tapeke – score (result of a game)

E rua ki te whā – Two to four
Kotahi rau ki te kotahi rau mā rua – 100 to 102
I tata – It was close

Ka mau te wehi!

Fantastic!

●

Here are some other exclamations that might be useful in this context.

Auahi ana! – How good was that!
Kātuarehe! – Outstanding!
Kei tawhiti! – Untouchable!

Kei te whakahīhī ahau i a koe.

I'm proud of you.

●

Whakahīhī is to be proud, in this context. However, *whakahīhī* can also mean to be arrogant or smug: *He whakahīhī a Tame* (Tame is arrogant).

Me whakanui tātou.

Let's celebrate.

●

whakanui – celebrate

Replace *whakanui* with:

whakangahau – have fun
pāti – party

26.

TE PUREI KĒMU

Playing games

He aha te kēmu?

What's the game?

●

Hī ika – Go fish
Maumahara – Memory
Kāri whakamutunga – Last card

Me pēhea te tākaro?

How do you play?

●

Mātaki mai – Watch (this)
Whai mai – Follow suit
Me pēnei – Like this

Mā wai e tīmata?

Who starts?

●

tīmata – to start

Māu – You will
Māku – I will
Mā te pōtiki – The youngest will

Kei a wai ināianei?

Whose turn now?

●

Kei ahau – It's mine
Kei a koe – It's yours
Kei a Ria – It's Ria's

Kāti te whakaroaroa.

Stop stalling.

●

Replace *whakaroaroa* with *kōrero* (talking), *tinihanga* (cheating) or *pēnā* (doing that).

Whiua ngā mataono.

Roll the dice.

●

whiu – to toss, throw

Mata (surface) and *ono* (six) makes 'dice'.

Tō waimarie hoki.

You're so lucky.

●

Replace *waimarie* with another adjective like *pōturi* (slow) or *kakama* (fast).

Kaua e tinihanga.

Don't cheat.

●

tinihanga – cheat

Replace *tinihanga* with *whātare* (peek), *pēnā* (do that) or *kata* (laugh).

Katikatihia ngā kāri.

Shuffle the cards.

●

kāri – card

The word *katikati* for 'shuffle' is derived from the
English word 'cut' (the cards).

Tohaina kia rima ki ia tangata.

Deal five to each person.

●

The suffix *-ina* turns the verb *toha* into a command. In this context *toha* means to distribute, share or deal (cards).

Tīkina he kāri.

Pick up a card.

●

Tīkina – Pick up
Tīkina kia rua – Pick up two
Tīkina kia rima – Pick up five

E hia ngā takirua kei a koe?

How many pairs do you have?

●

takirua – pair

Respond with:

E whitu kei ahau – I have seven
E hia kei a koe? – How many do you have?

Ko au te toa!

I'm the winner!

●

Ko koe te toa! – You're the winner!
Ko Cora te toa! – Cora's the winner!

27.

NGĀ KARE Ā-ROTO

Feelings and emotions

Ka nui taku aroha ki a koe.

I love you very much.

●

aroha – love

Ka nui te aroha can mean 'much love'.

Kua wera taku poho.

I'm turned on.

●

poho – chest

This literally says, 'my chest is burning', expressing excitement.

Kei te tino harikoa ahau.

I'm elated.

●

Swap *harikoa* (happy) with another state, such as *pōuri* (sad), *hiakai* (hungry) or *ora* (well).

I rutua ahau e te mataku.

I was overcome with fear.

●

Mataku (fear) may also be swapped out for another noun like *whakamā* (embarrassment), *riri* (anger) or *hiamoe* (sleepiness).

E whakamomori ana ahau ki a koe.

I miss you dearly.

●

Whakamomori can also mean to commit suicide.
In the past, the act of pining, fretting or missing
someone desperately, especially someone who had
passed away, might have led to someone taking their
own life.

Kaua e whakamau.

Don't hold a grudge.

●

whakamau – hold a grudge

Replace *whakamau* with:

pāmamae – take offence
mate wheke – give in
tangi – cry

He aha ia i kiripiro mai ai?

Why is he/she being cold towards me?

●

kiripiro – to dislike

Remember, *ia* is a gender-neutral pronoun for the third person and can mean 'he/him' or 'she/her'.

Kaua e riri kurī noa.

Don't get angry for nothing.

●

Kurī after a verb indicates that the speaker believes the action is unwarranted, pointless or just a pretence.

Kua hōhā au i tēnei.

I'm over this.

●

hōhā – fed up with

Kua hōhā au i a koe! – Well, I'm over you!

Kāti te tangimeme.

Stop crying.

●

Tangimeme (to fret, cry) is also a noun: *He tangimeme koe* (You're a crybaby).

He aha koe e pōuri nā?

Why are you sad?

●

pōuri – sad

You might respond with:

Nā te mea – Because
Kaua e pātai – Don't ask

E hokirua ana ngā whakaaro.

I'm not sure about this.

●

hokirua – to be doubtful, unsure, uncertain

Kua rangirua aku mahara is another phrase you can use to say you're unsure or confused about something. *Rangirua* literally means 'two skies', which indicates being in two minds about something.

Kei te māharahara ahau ki a koe.

I'm worried about you.

●

For some reason there are a lot of words for 'worried' in Māori – *āwangawanga, mānukanuka, mānatunatu, whakaririka* – just to name a few.

28.

TE MĀUIUI

Sickness

Kei te māuiui ahau.

I'm not feeling well.

●

māuiui – to be sick, unwell (verb); sickness (noun)

The *uiui* in *māuiui* is pronounced almost the same as *wiwi*. Roll the *u* and *i* together quickly.

He aha te mate?

What's wrong?

●

Mate is another word for sickness or illness.

Kei te ānini taku upoko – I have a headache
Kei te ngau taku puku – I have a stomach ache

Kei whea e mamae ana?

Where does it hurt?

●

mamae – hurt, pain

Here are some body parts:

upoko – head
tuarā – back
waewae – leg
ringaringa – arm, hand
puku – stomach

Kua whara tōku waewae.

I've hurt my leg.

●

whara – injured, hurt

Here are some body parts:

waewae – leg, foot
ringa – arm
matimati – finger
pokohiwi – shoulder

Whakaatuhia mai.

Show me.

●

Māku e kihi – I'll kiss it
Māku e whakatika – I'll make it better
Māku e uhi ki te piriora – I'll put a plaster on it

Kua katirehe taku korokoro.

My throat is sore.

●

korokoro – throat

It's important to note that *katirehe* is only used for a sore throat – not for any other part of the body.

Whētero mai tō arero.

Poke your tongue out.

●

arero – tongue

Whētero is the act of poking out the tongue, made famous by the men's *pūkana* in the *haka*.

Kia titiro atu ahau.

Let me take a look.

●

Kia kaha – Be strong
Kia toa – Be brave
Kia manawanui – Be patient

Kia tau te noho.

Sit still.

●

Kaua e kori – Don't wriggle

Kaua e tangi – Don't cry

Kaua e koemi – Don't flinch

Kua pā mai te rewharewha.

I've come down with the flu.

●

rewharewha – flu

Replace *rewharewha* with:

maremare – cough
ihu pāwera – hay fever
harehare – eczema, skin ailment

Kāore au e kaha ki te haere ki te mahi.

I'm not fit to go to work.

•

Note this one for future correspondence with your *rangatira* if you're *māuiui* and won't make it to *mahi*.

Ka haere au ki te tākuta āpōpō.

I'll go to the doctor tomorrow.

●

tākuta – doctor

Replace *tākuta* with:

nēhi – nurse
hōhipera – hospital

Kia piki te ora.

Get well.

●

ora – to be well (verb); health, wellbeing (noun)

Here are my recovery tips:

inu wai – drink water
whakatā – rest
rongoā – medicine

A Māori Word a Day:
365 Words to Kickstart your Reo

Hēmi Kelly

An incredibly simple, fun and practical Māori dictionary for all New Zealanders.

A Māori Word a Day offers an easy entry into the Māori language. Through its 365 Māori words, you will learn:

- Definitions and word types
- Fun facts and background information
- Sample sentences, in both te reo Māori and English

Exploring the most common and contemporary words in use today, *A Māori Word a Day* is the perfect way to kickstart your reo journey!

'A great tool for anyone wanting to learn the Māori language.'
—*Linda Hall, Hawke's Bay Weekend*

Sleeps Standing:
A Story of the Battle of Ōrākau

Witi Ihimaera, Hēmi Kelly

Both fiction and fact, this is a kaleidoscopic exploration of the Battle of Ōrākau.

During three days in 1864, 300 Māori men, women and children fought an imperial army and captured the imagination of the world.

Instead of following the victors, this book offers varied Māori perspectives, centring on Witi Ihimaera's moving novella, *Sleeps Standing*, featuring a boy named Moetū. Further giving voice to and illuminating the people who tried to protect their culture and land are Māori eyewitness accounts, images and a Māori translation by Hēmi Kelly.

Selected as one of the '100 Best Books of 2017'
—*New Zealand Listener*

Te Rātaka a Tama Hūngoingoi:
Diary of a Wimpy Kid

Jeff Kinney

In this brilliant translation of Jeff Kinney's bestselling *Diary of a Wimpy Kid*, by Hēni Jacob, 12-year-old hero Greg Heffley is the Tama Hūngoingoi (Wimpy Kid).

A great book in any language, *Te Rātaka a Tama Hūngoingoi* is packed with laughter, gags, disasters, daydreams and plenty to keep young readers hooked until the very end.

My First Words in Māori

Stacey Morrison

Illustrated by Ali Teo and John O'Reilly

If you'd like to speak the beautiful Māori language with your kids, this is the book to get you started!

My First Words in Māori equips your whānau with the first words you need to speak te reo at home together.

Written by Māori language champion and broadcaster Stacey Morrison for parents and tamariki to read together, with lively pictures labelled in Māori and English, each page introduces the concepts and words children use as they first begin to talk, get to know people and explore the world around them. Reflecting the faces and places of Aotearoa, *My First Words in Māori* is a must-have for homes and classrooms.

Māori Made Easy:
For everyday learners of the Māori language

Scotty Morrison

Scotty Morrison's *Māori Made Easy* is the one-stop resource for anyone wanting to learn the basics of the Māori language.

Māori Made Easy allows the reader to take control of their learning in an empowering way. By committing just 30 minutes a day for 30 weeks, learners will adopt the language easily and as best suits their busy lives.

Written by popular TV personality and te reo Māori advocate Scotty Morrison, this book proves that learning the language can be fun, effective – and easy!

'This is not just a useful book, it's an essential one.'
—*Paul Little, North & South*

Winner of Ngā Kupu Ora Māori Book Awards 2016.
(Te Reo Māori – Māori Language)

Māori at Home:
An everyday guide to learning the Māori language

Scotty and Stacey Morrison

The accessible and fun guide for everyday Kiwis looking to learn and speak the Māori language around the home.

Māori at Home is the perfect introduction to the Māori language. A highly practical, easy and fun resource for everyday New Zealanders, it covers the basics of life in and around a typical Kiwi household.

Whether you're practising sport, getting ready for school, celebrating a birthday, preparing a shopping list or relaxing at the beach, *Māori at Home* gives you the words and phrases – and confidence – you need.

'This is the book you want – for your family, for your kids, for yourself.' —*The Spinoff*

Māori at Work:
The everyday guide to using te reo Māori in the workplace

Scotty Morrison

A simple, practical and engaging guide to using the Māori language in and around your workplace.

Māori at Work offers phrases and tips for greetings and welcoming people, emails and letters, speeches and social media, with specific chapters on the office, construction and roadworks, retail, hospitality, broadcasting and teaching.

This is the perfect book to start or expand their te reo journey – no matter your skill level!

The Raupō Phrasebook of Modern Māori:
The user-friendly guide for all New Zealanders

Scotty Morrison

The Raupō Phrasebook of Modern Māori is the most up-to-date, versatile and relevant resource for using Māori language in everyday life.

Whether you're a novice or emergent speaker of te reo Māori, or a complete beginner, you'll learn useful phrases for the home, the marae, the workplace, meeting and greeting, eating and drinking and so much more!

'Clever but written in a user-friendly style... an important little book for all New Zealanders interested in te reo.'
—*Katherine Findlay, Mana*